TODDLERS' DEVOTIONAL
MADE SIMPLE

EMILY QUAINOO

FriesenPress

One Printers Way
Altona, MB R0G 0B0
Canada

www.friesenpress.com

First Edition — 2022

ISBN
978-1-03-914170-4 (Hardcover)
978-1-03-914168-8 (Paperback)
978-1-03-914171-1 (eBook)

1. *Juvenile Nonfiction, Religious, Christian, Devotional & Prayer*

Distributed to the trade by The Ingram Book Company

DEDICATION

This toddlers' devotion is lovingly dedicated to my two beautiful granddaughters, Avery and Anaya.

ACKNOWLEDGEMENT

I thank the Almighty God for the knowledge, grace and strength He is given me to develop this material. To my husband James, and our children Beryllia, Daniel, and Kwabena, thank you for encouraging me to put this devotional material together. I also wish to appreciate my dearest sisters, Joyce Arthur and Agnes Ansong for their support.

To everyone else who supported me directly and indirectly, I am eternally grateful. God richly bless you all.

INTRODUCTION

As a young grandmother, I love to sing and pray with my granddaughters every night before they go to bed. We read stories from scriptures and other books, and we pray together. Several of the scriptures we read together are included in this devotional. They inspired me to put this devotional together.

Children must be encouraged to read and listen to good stories right from birth. They also need to be encouraged to pray by themselves, thus, instilling in them the need and power of prayer.

Prayer helps children to discover the ultimate source of all help and strength as they grow.

People were bringing little children to Jesus for him to place his hands on them, but the disciples rebuked them. When Jesus saw this, he was indignant. He said to them, "Let the little children come to me, and do not hinder them, for the kingdom of God belongs to such as these." Mark 10:13-16

I trust that all who come into contact with this devotional will find it beneficial and a helpful teaching resource that can help children connect to the divine.

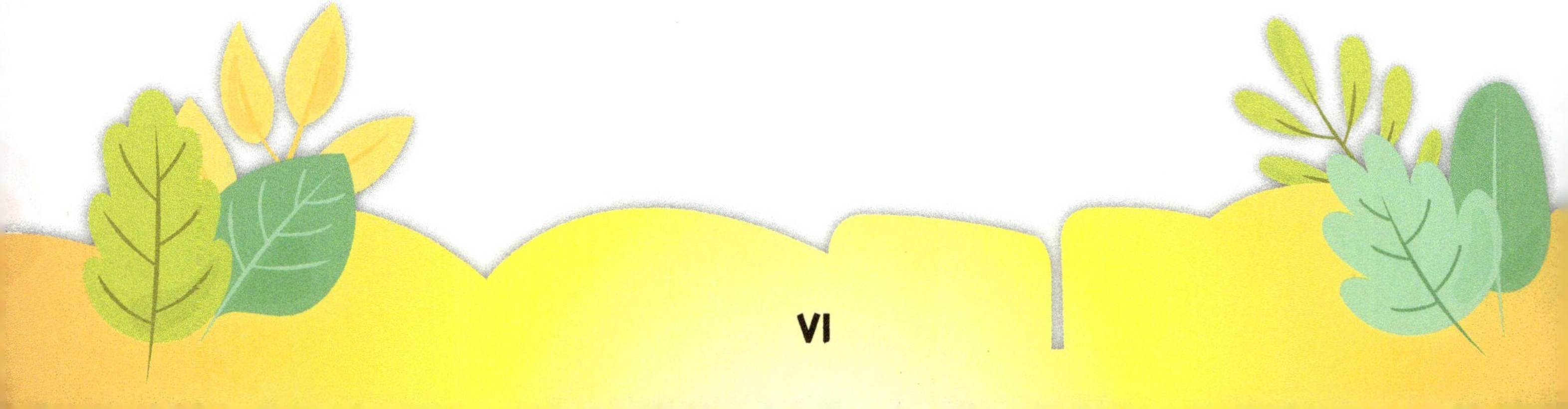

"Behold, children are a heritage from the LORD, the fruit of the womb is a reward."
Psalms 127:3

1
CREATION

GOD CREATED THE HEAVENS AND THE EARTH
GENESIS 1:1

God is the Creator.
God created me, Mom, Dad and my friends.
God created the birds, fish, and all the animals.
God made the sky, moon, sun
and all the trees.
God made all things.

PRAYER

DEAR GOD, THANK YOU FOR MAKING ALL THINGS, INCLUDING ME. AMEN.

2
OBEY

CHILDREN OBEY YOUR PARENTS.
EPHESIANS 6:1

To obey is to listen to Mom and Dad
and do what they say.
To obey is to listen to your teachers
and follow all they teach.
To obey is to listen to the word of God and do his will.
Jesus listened to his Father and did what he said.
I must listen to Mom and Dad.

PRAYER

LORD JESUS, PLEASE HELP ME TO LISTEN AND DO YOUR WILL. AMEN.

3
REJOICE

REJOICE IN THE LORD.
PHILIPPIANS 4:4

To rejoice is to be happy.

I am happy when I am singing and dancing.
I am happy when my sister plays with me.
I feel happy when grandma buys me a  toy.

PRAYER

DEAR JESUS, THANK YOU FOR MAKING ME HAPPY TODAY. AMEN.

4

FEAR

DO NOT BE AFRAID.
ISAIAH 43:5

Fear is the feeling we get when
we are scared of something.
I am not scared, because Mom is with me.
I am not scared, because Jesus is my friend.
He is always around to keep me safe.

PRAYER

LORD JESUS, THANK YOU FOR KEEPING ME SAFE AT ALL TIMES. AMEN.

5
STEALING

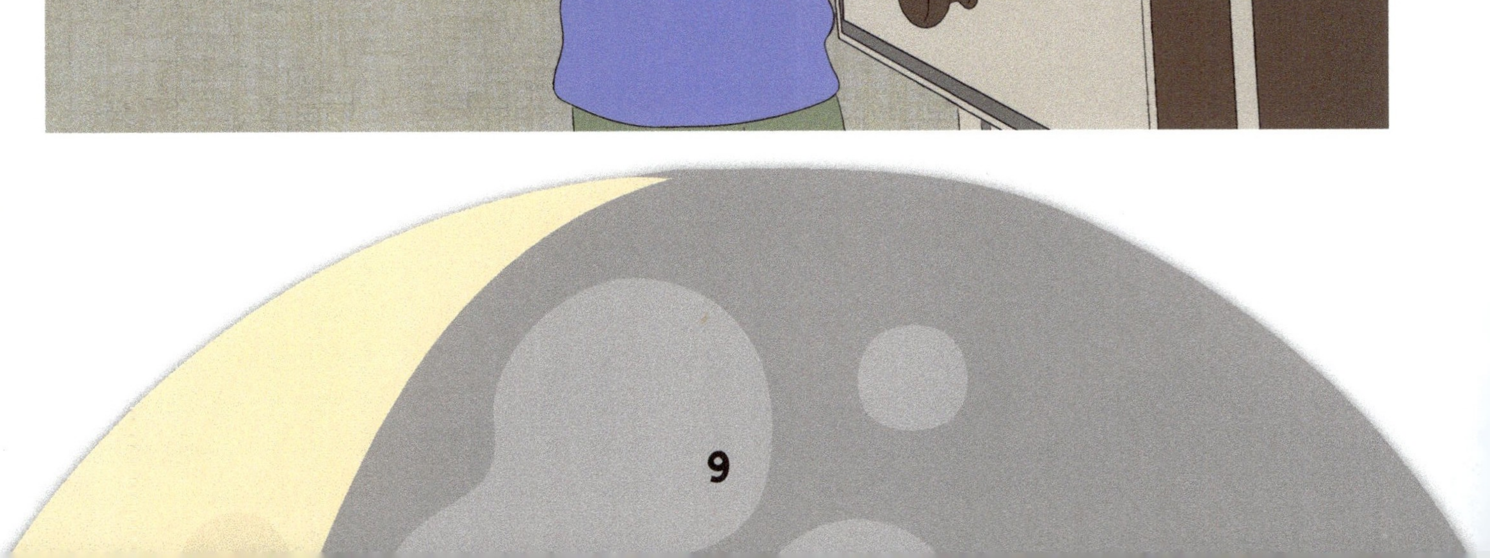

DO NOT STEAL.
LEVITICUS 19:11

Do not take anything that is not yours
and pretend it is yours.
Do not pick your friend's toy and say, "it is mine."
Jesus does not want us to take anything that does
not belong to us.
We must always ask first.

PRAYERS

LORD JESUS, PLEASE HELP ME TO BE HAPPY WITH MY TOYS AND NEVER TAKE MY FRIEND'S TOYS WITHOUT ASKING. AMEN.

6
LYING

DO NOT LIE.
LEVITICUS 19:11

Do not say anything that is not true.
Always speak the truth just as it is.
If you took the cookies, say, “I took the cookies.”
If you took the candy, say, “I took the candy.”

PRAYERS

DEAR LORD JESUS, PLEASE HELP ME TO SPEAK THE TRUTH ALWAYS. AMEN.

7
SHINING

LET YOUR LIGHT SHINE.
MATTHEW 5:16

The Sun is the light for the day.
It shines in the morning so we can see.
The Moon is the light for the night.
It brightens the night, so we do not fall.
Jesus is my light, so he makes me shine.

PRAYER

DEAR JESUS, PLEASE MAKE MY LIGHT SHINE. AMEN.

8

CARING

...BECAUSE HE CARES FOR YOU.
1 PETER 5:7

Caring is making someone feel special.
Caring is saying kind words to others.
Mom makes me feel special as she baths
and dresses me nicely.
Dad makes me feel special as he says, “I love you,”
and “You are wonderful.”
Jesus makes me feel special as he cares for me.

PRAYER

LORD JESUS, PLEASE HELP ME TO CARE FOR OTHERS AS YOU CARE FOR ME. AMEN.

9
9 KINDNESS

BE KIND ...TO ONE ANOTHER.
EPHESIANS 4:32

Kindness is being nice to another person.
To be kind is to give to others
without expecting anything back.
Mom and Dad are always nice to me.
They give me what I need.
I am always nice to my friends.
Jesus is always kind to me.

PRAYER

LORD JESUS, I THANK YOU FOR BEING KIND TO ME. AMEN.

10
LOVE

LOVE YOUR NEIGHBOR AS YOURSELF.
MATTHEW 22:39

To love is to care for others.
To love is to give to the people around you.
To love is to be fair.
To love is not cheating your friends.
To love is to share my toys with my friends. Jesus loves all of us and he gives to all of us.

PRAYERS

DEAR JESUS, PLEASE HELP ME TO LOVE EVERYONE. AMEN.

11
TRUST

TRUST IN THE LORD WITH ALL YOUR HEART.
PROVERBS 3:5

Trust is believing in something.

I trust Mom because she feeds me
anytime I need to eat.
I trust Dad because he puts me to bed.
I trust Jesus because He is always with me.

PRAYERS

DEAR JESUS, THANK YOU FOR ALWAYS BEING WITH ME. AMEN.

12
BELIEVE

BELIEVE ON THE LORD JESUS CHRIST.
ACT 16:31

To believe is to accept that something is true.
To believe is knowing that someone is able to do something.
I believe that God can do all things.
I believe that Jesus is the son of God.
I believe that Jesus is my savior.
I believe that Jesus loves me, and I love him too.

PRAYERS

LORD JESUS, THANK YOU FOR BEING MY SAVIOR. AMEN.

CONCLUSION

But you, Lord, are forever exalted.

Psalm 92:8

Printed in the USA
CPSIA information can be obtained
at www.ICGtesting.com
JSHW070249071123
51581JS00005B/16

9 781039 141698